D1489334

DATE DUE

	DISCARD		
GAYLORD			PRINTED IN U.S.A.

Extraordinary
Horseshoe Crabs

Extraordinary Horseshoe Crabs

by Julie Dunlap
A Carolrhoda Nature Watch Book

Carolrhoda Books, Inc. / Minneapolis

To Kathy, Katy, and Kali—extraordinary friends.

My sincere appreciation to Tom O'Connell, Carl Shuster Jr., William Hall, Karen Williams, Robert Barlow, and Chris Passaglia for sharing their expertise. Special thanks also to Mary and Joe Vogel and Marybeth Lorbiecki for their generous assistance and support.

Carolrhoda Books, Inc., c/o The Lerner Publishing Group 241 First Avenue North, Minneapolis, MN 55401 U.S.A.

Website address: www.lernerbooks.com

LIBRARY OF CONGRESS CATALOGING-IN-PUBLICATION DATA

Dunlap, Julie.
  Extraordinary horseshoe crabs / by Julie Dunlap.
    p.   cm.
  "A Carolrhoda nature watch book."
  Includes index.
  Summary: Describes the physical characteristics, habits, life cycle, and conservation of horseshoe crabs.
    ISBN 1-57505-293-8 (alk. paper)
    1. Limulus polyphemus—Juvenile literature.
[1. Horseshoe crabs.] I. Title.
QL447.7.D85   1999
595.4'92—dc21   98-6990

Manufactured in the United States of America
1 2 3 4 5 6 — JR — 04 03 02 01 00 99

FOR MORE INFORMATION
on efforts to study and protect
horseshoe crabs, write to:

Cape May Bird Observatory
600 Route 47 North
Cape May Court House, NJ 08210

CONTENTS

EXTRA-ORDINARY

Each spring, brown, helmet-like shells appear on beaches along North America's Atlantic Coast. Most beachcombers, looking for rare and delicate seashells, don't give the creatures a second glance. After all, they're just ordinary horseshoe crabs.

If people notice horseshoe crabs at all, they often call the animals dull, worthless, or just plain ugly. It's true that there's nothing cuddly about the horseshoes' tough, horny shells. They look about as exciting as wet rocks lying on the sand. Even worse, when lots of dead horseshoes pile up on a beach, they stink! They're common and troublesome, many people think. Just useless pests.

A horseshoe crab may look ordinary on the outside, but scientists have discovered that the horseshoe is an extraordinary animal—it has blue blood, a mouth between its legs, and eyes scattered around its body.

But scientists who study horseshoe crabs are making startling discoveries about them. What other "ordinary" animal has blue blood, a mouth between its legs, and eyes scattered around its body? What other living creature looks so much like its ancient relatives, which lived before the first dinosaurs? And most amazing, what other "useless pest" is so important to the health of human beings and the lives of many kinds of wildlife?

Only the horseshoe crab.

Though there are four **species,** or kinds, of horseshoe crabs in the world, this book will focus mainly on the one North American species, known to scientists as *Limulus polyphemus.* As you read, you may discover that horseshoe crabs aren't ordinary after all.

From ancient fossils like this one, which is 155 million years old, we see that horseshoe crabs have changed very little in millions of years.

HORSESHOE TICKS

If you could travel through time, back 360 million years, you would find animals remarkably like our horseshoe crabs.

Called xiphosurans (which is Greek for "sword-tailed ones"), the ancient horseshoe relatives crawled along the sandy seafloor over 100 million years before the first dinosaurs appeared. The earth has changed much over the millions of years since that time. Many lifeforms, including the dinosaurs, have become **extinct,** or died out.

Most species of plants and animals that managed to survive changed little by little over millions of years—a process known as **evolution.** The xiphosurans that survived, however, appear to have changed very little. In fact, horseshoe crabs look so similar to their long-ago ancestors that people often call them "living fossils." (Fossils are shells or other traces of long-dead plants and animals that have hardened into rock.)

True crabs, like this Atlantic blue crab (above), *are only distant relatives of the horseshoe crab* (right).

When early European explorers wrote about a sword-tailed beast in North America, many called it "King Crabb." Later it somehow gained the name "horsefoot," probably after the outline of its shell, which looks like a horse's hoof. But most people now use the name "horseshoe crab."

Strangely enough, horseshoes are not really crabs at all. A true crab, such as an Atlantic blue crab, has two pairs of antennae, or feelers, and a pair of jaws on its head. Examine a horseshoe crab, and you'll find it has no antennae. Also, its mouth is a jawless slit between its legs. Such differences show that horseshoes and true crabs are only distant relatives.

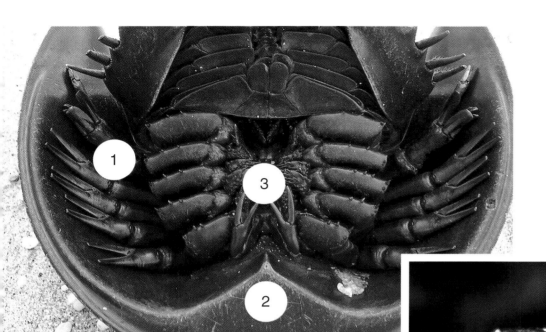

The underside of a horseshoe crab (above) *shows the jointed legs* (1) *and hard outer covering* (2) *that place it in a group of animals called arthropods. The horseshoe crab also has a pair of feeding pincers* (3) *to help it grasp food just as spiders do* (right).

If it isn't a crab, then what is it?

Like true crabs, as well as spiders and insects, horseshoe crabs belong to a huge group of animals called **arthropods.** Arthropods don't have backbones or skeletons made of bones like we do. But arthropods do have jointed legs and hard outer coverings that protect their soft bodies.

Scientists group different kinds of arthropods according to traits they have in common. In front of each horseshoe's mouth slit is a pair of **chelicerae** (kih-LIH-seh-REE), or feeding pincers. A horseshoe uses these handy grippers to grasp worms and other food.

The only other arthropods with these unique tools are horseshoes' closest living relatives: ticks, spiders, and scorpions. But there are many important differences—such as the spiky tail—between horseshoes and their crawling cousins. So "horseshoe tick" would not have made a better name. Instead, horseshoe crabs were placed in a class of their own—Merostomata.

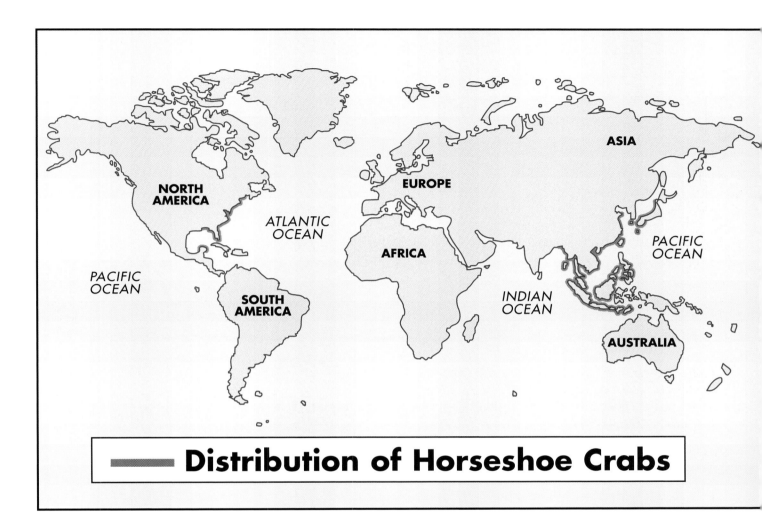

Distribution of Horseshoe Crabs

Fossil hunters have discovered rock-hard evidence of hundreds of species that would also fit in the class Merostomata. No one knows why, but all of the giant water scorpions and most of the other species in Merostomata died out long ago. Just four species of horseshoe crab still exist.

Horseshoes spend their lives burrowing through the mud and crawling along the bottoms of oceans and saltwater bays, coming ashore only to mate. Three species live in the Pacific and Indian Oceans, along the coasts of Japan, China, Indonesia, the Philippines, and India. The fourth kind—*Limulus polyphemus*—lives in many places along the western shores of the Atlantic Ocean, from Maine to Florida, plus Mexico's Yucatán Peninsula.

A CLOSER LOOK

The first thing people usually notice about horseshoe crabs is their shells. Like other arthropods, horseshoes sport outer coverings that protect the animals like suits of armor. The main ingredient of that body armor is a tough, horny substance called **chitin** (KY-tin). A true crab's chitin-rich shell is thin and brittle, but a horseshoe shell is flexible, like a very thick fingernail.

Scary-looking to some people, the horseshoe's sturdy covering shields it from most **predators**, or animals that might like to eat it. In addition, the armor helps keep the horseshoe from drying out when it crawls onshore.

The hardness of the horseshoe's tough, spiny shell (above right) protects it from most predators. But it must beware of the loggerhead turtle (right). The turtle's powerful jaws can easily tear into a chitin shell and eat the horseshoe.

It's easy to tell which of these mating horseshoe crabs is the male and which is the female. Full-grown females can be almost twice the size of males.

In rough surf, the shell's rounded shape helps keep the animal from flipping over. Also, the curved shell allows a horseshoe to plow like a miniature bulldozer through the undersea mud, muck, and sand in search of buried food.

Not all horseshoe shells look identical. The most noticeable difference in shells is between those of males and females. Adult females can be almost twice as big as males! Full-grown females are about 2 feet (0.6 m) long, including the tail. A horseshoe's size also depends on its age, with the biggest, oldest females weighing up to 10 pounds (4.5 kg).

Shell colors vary, too—more than you might expect. Young horseshoes living around the Delaware Bay are often green brown, while older ones are usually dark brown. Horseshoe crabs found in southern Florida can be almost as pale as cream.

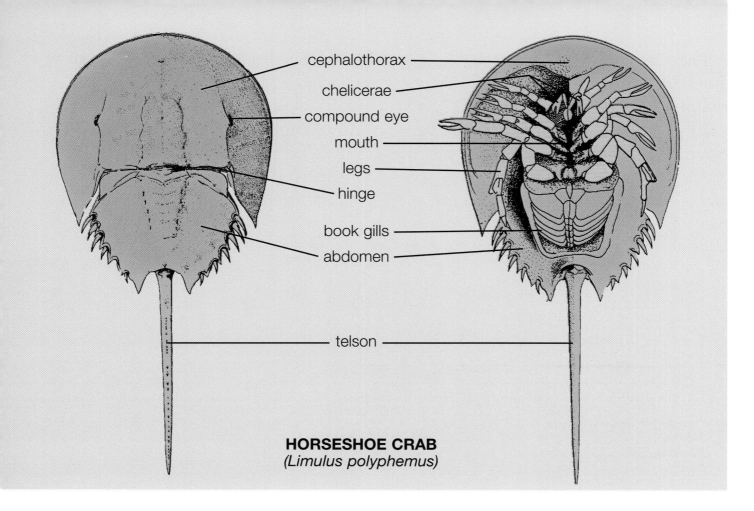

cephalothorax

chelicerae

compound eye

mouth

legs

hinge

book gills

abdomen

telson

HORSESHOE CRAB
(Limulus polyphemus)

Horseshoe crabs have three main body parts. The front part, shaped like a horse's hoof, is called the **cephalothorax** (sef-e-le-THOR-aks), and the smaller, triangular midsection is the **abdomen.** The first two body parts are connected by a strong hinge that lets the animal bend sharply in the middle. (Beware—fingers caught in the bend can get a painful pinch.) This hinge allows horseshoes to do a kind of bend-flip, bend-flip swimming motion.

The horseshoe's third body part is a sharp-pointed tail, or **telson.** Despite its scary looks, the telson is not a weapon for killing other animals for food. The telson won't hurt you—unless you step on it barefoot. Horseshoe crabs use their telsons to help plow through the mud for food. A hungry horseshoe pushes with its legs, bends at its hinge, and swings its telson side to side, sweeping away the mud, to dig deeper, faster.

14

The telson can also save the horseshoe's life. If a heavy wave flips the animal onto its back, it is in trouble. Beach stranding is probably nature's number-one killer of adult horseshoe crabs. The broiling sun dries and weakens the animal. Then herring gulls, raccoons, or other beach predators can make an easy meal of the tired horseshoe—too weak to bend, thrash about, or thrust out its spiky tail.

Luckily, an upside-down horseshoe can thrust its telson into the sand to help flip itself right side up. But horseshoes with broken telsons or damaged tail muscles may swing their tails, bend their bodies, and thrash their legs for hours without flipping over.

When on its back, a horseshoe crab uses its telson to help flip itself upright (top left). Never pick up a horseshoe by the telson; a broken telson could cripple the animal and even lead to its death. If a horseshoe cannot flip right side up, it closes its hinge and pinches itself together, trying to protect its soft body (left).

15

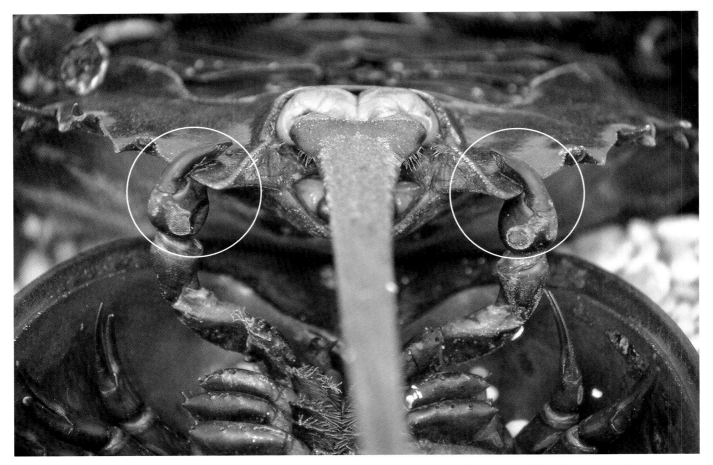

When mating, a male horseshoe crab uses special claws (circled) shaped like boxing gloves to hold onto the back edge of a female.

For a closer look at the underside, firmly grasp the front of the shell and turn the horseshoe over (it won't bite!). The first small pincers you see on the cephalothorax are the small chelicerae (feeding grippers) that horseshoes share with spiders, ticks, and scorpions.

Next come five pairs of walking legs. The back pair of legs are extra long and tipped with fanlike structures that aid in burrowing. In young horseshoes and adult females, the other four pairs of legs end in claws for holding food. In adult males, though, the first two legs are tipped with special claws called **claspers.** Males use their claspers to hold onto females during mating. Shaped like boxing gloves, these claspers make it easy to tell males from females.

16

A horseshoe crab searches the seafloor for food.

Between the legs is a slit, which is the horseshoe's mouth, complete without jaws or teeth. To find food, a hungry horseshoe plows slowly along the seafloor (crawling forward, not sideways like a blue crab does), its chelicerae probing the muck for food. Horseshoes aren't picky—they'll eat almost anything, from algae to dead fish. But their favorite foods are marine worms and small clams.

How does a horseshoe crab chew without jaws or teeth? Believe it or not, by moving its legs. A horseshoe's claws push each meal between its legs. There, at the base of the legs, are short, heavy spines. The animal moves its legs, and the spines crush the food into bite-sized bits. Just imagine—horseshoe crabs "chew" their dinners between their legs!

Horseshoes use gills, located on the underside of the abdomen, to breathe.

You may wonder how a horseshoe finds worms, clams, and other food it likes to eat under mud on the dark bay floor. The chelicerae discover food by touch. Sensitive bristles on the legs may also help. Some scientists think the bristles detect chemicals in the water given off by the things horseshoes like to eat. So even though horseshoes lack noses, they may find snacks by chemical "smells."

Behind the legs and mouth, on the underside of the horseshoe's abdomen, a leatherlike flap covers five pairs of **gills,** or breathing organs. Like fish, a horseshoe breathes with gills instead of lungs. However, a horseshoe's gills are different from those of any other living animal. Each of the 10 gills holds a stack of about 100 sheets of tissue that resemble the pages of a book.

To breathe, the horseshoe crab flaps its **book gills,** forcing water past the pages. Oxygen in the water passes through the gills and into the horseshoe's blood. If stranded out of water, a horseshoe crab digs itself into the wet sand. It can breathe for days as long as its gills stay damp.

So horseshoe crabs breathe without lungs, may "smell" without noses, and can chew without jaws. Do they see without eyes?

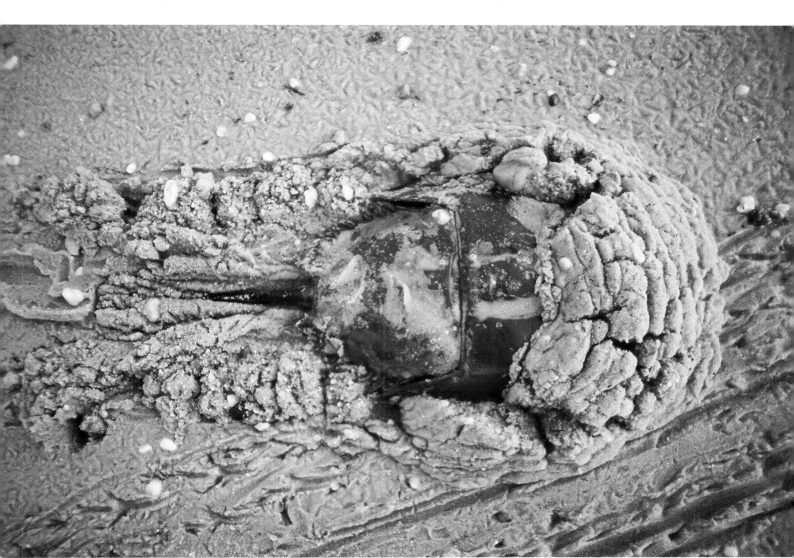

A horseshoe crab burrows into wet sand to keep its gills damp when it is out of the water.

Limulus polyphemus is named after a one-eyed giant, Polyphemus, from Greek mythology (*limulus* means "a sideways glance" in Latin). In the past, scientists believed that horseshoes' eyes were almost useless. What could the animals see, anyway, in the murky deep?

Researchers have since discovered that a horseshoe crab sees in several different ways and that it has ten "eyes." None of the eyes looks or sees much like ours. The two eyes on the underside and five of the eyes on top probably can't see images, but they can tell light from dark. Two of the small eyes on top can even sense ultraviolet light, which people can't see at all. Another "eye" is actually a collection of **photoreceptors,** or cells that are sensitive to light. This group of photoreceptors lies along the telson.

The horseshoe's most noticeable eyes are the two large **compound eyes** peering out from either side of the cephalothorax. Each of these compound eyes is made up of about 1,000 photoreceptors. But even 1,000 photoreceptors are not enough to allow horseshoes to make out clear images. Our own sharp eyes contain over 100 million photoreceptors each.

The images horseshoes see are blurry and black and white. But horseshoes can make out movements and shapes of objects to the front, to the side, and even behind them.

A large female horseshoe digs into the sand (above). Horseshoes have two compound eyes, located on either side of the cephalothorax (inset). The photoreceptors in these eyes are the largest yet discovered in any animal. Because the receptors are so large, they are easier to study than receptors in other animals.

Dr. Barlow and other researchers placed female-sized cement models of horseshoe crabs (below) *in the water. Male horseshoes crawled to the models* (right).

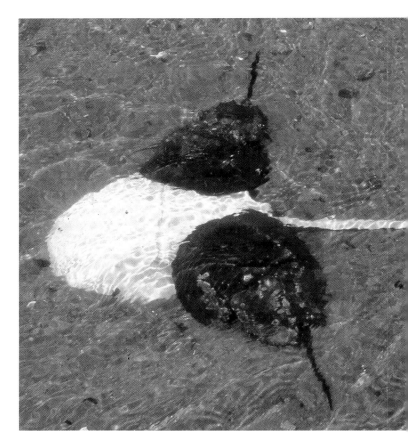

But what are horseshoes looking at? They don't need eyes to find food, and their shells protect them from most predators. Dr. Robert Barlow, a vision researcher, thought horseshoes might use their eyes to find mates. But other scientists believed males follow scent clues given off by females. So Dr. Barlow and other researchers tested their ideas by placing female-sized cement models on the sea bottom.

Male horseshoes within three or four feet crawled directly toward the models, though they smelled more like cement than horseshoe crabs. The experiment showed that male horseshoes see at least well enough to recognize the shape of a female.

Amazingly, it didn't matter whether it was night or day—the males still approached the models from the same distance. How could the animals see so well in the dark water? Horseshoes have yet another incredible ability: their eyesight adjusts from day to night.

To study a horseshoe-eye view of the world, researchers mount tiny cameras on top of live horseshoes. Then researchers analyze the "crab-cam" videos by computer, looking for more clues about how the horseshoes' eyes work.

Around sunset, the animal's brain sends a message to its compound eyes, causing the photoreceptors to become up to a *million* times more sensitive to light. They are so sensitive, in fact, that mate-finding on moonlit nights is almost as easy as on sunny afternoons. Then, as the sun rises, the horseshoe brain turns the eyes' light sensitivity back down again. These changes in the eyes are part of a daily cycle similar to the human pattern of waking and sleeping.

Scientists aren't quite sure how the whole process works, but they suspect the light-sensitive "eye" on the telson may have some part to play. Many other questions about horseshoe vision remain (such as how they use the small eyes on the top of their shells and why they have eyes on their undersides), so researchers continue to experiment. Some have even attached miniature video cameras to live horseshoes to analyze more thoroughly what horseshoe crabs see.

One thing is certain, however—the "useless" eyes of a horseshoe male work well enough to find a female, day or night.

BRAND-NEW HORSESHOES

At first, the only sound on the calm May night comes from gentle waves lapping on soft sand. A full moon brightens the Delaware Bay beach, with moonlight glinting off the wet backs of a few horseshoe crabs scattered along the water's edge. The first *Limuli* to appear are followed by dozens more, then by hundreds, then thousands.

By high tide, eerie sounds rise above the quiet waves—*crunch, scrape, creak*. These are the sounds of shells grating against shells, as horseshoe crabs scrabble over horseshoe crabs on their way up the beach. Anyone lucky enough to witness this age-old scene agrees—it is unforgettable.

Horseshoe crabs crowd a beach on the New Jersey side of Delaware Bay to mate and nest. Long stretches of sandy beaches and mild waves make Delaware Bay a popular place for nesting.

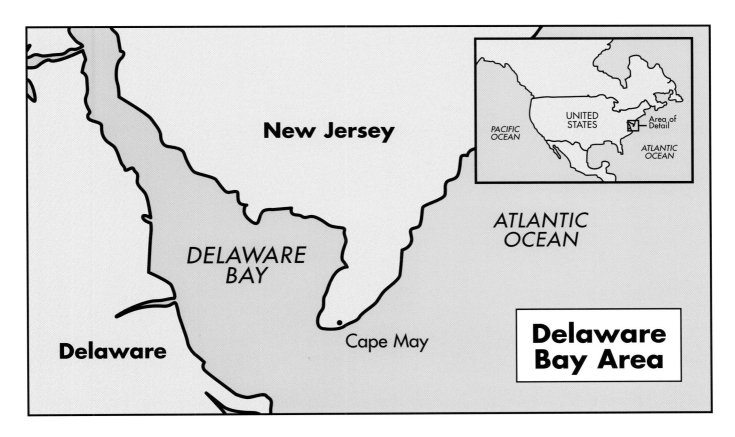

New Jersey

DELAWARE BAY

ATLANTIC OCEAN

Delaware

Cape May

Delaware Bay Area

UNITED STATES

PACIFIC OCEAN

Area of Detail

ATLANTIC OCEAN

During spring and early summer, you may chance upon *Limuli* on many North American beaches: Massachusetts's Cape Cod, Virginia's Assateague Island, or the Florida Keys, to name a few. But to see throngs of horseshoes, visit Delaware Bay. Dr. Carl Shuster, a world-famous horseshoe expert, estimates that over 50 percent of Atlantic Ocean horseshoes nest there, along the New Jersey and Delaware coasts.

Adult horseshoes spend their winters offshore, burrowing in the mud under the cold waters of bays and the deeper ocean. But in early spring, the longer days, warmer water temperatures, and perhaps other, more mysterious cues act like a wake-up alarm. Then the horseshoes crawl from the depths toward Delaware Bay and other nesting beaches.

Nesting has been seen any time between April and August, but on Delaware Bay, most horseshoes head beachward in May or June. The urge to nest seems strongest on late May and early June nights during spring tides (the higher-than-normal tides that occur with each full and new moon).

Six males surround a female as she digs a shallow nest for her eggs.

Males often find the beach first, pacing in the shallow water like kids awaiting a school bus. Not long before high tide, females begin to arrive. Several males surround each female, jostling each other to get close. Each male tries to grasp a female with his special claspers. Then he hangs on tight, and other males may clasp onto him, or onto the female's sides, one after another. One female may drag six or more males up the watery slope to nest.

Horseshoe crabs nest in the **intertidal zone,** a band of wave-washed sand between the high and low tide lines. The female digs with her legs and shell, scooping out a shallow, sandy bowl near the water's edge. She drops about 4,000 eggs, in golf-ball-sized clusters, inside.

Left: *Nesting horseshoes leave tracks in the sand as they crawl up and down the beach.*
Above: *A golf-ball-sized cluster of eggs*

At the same time, the male horseshoe crabs are releasing sperm into the water. The eggs are fertilized when the sperm washes over them.

With her job complete, the female crawls away, often with males still in tow. Waves will cover this first nest with sand, while the female may go on to dig several more nests that night, following the waterline up or down the beach. She may crawl ashore three or more times in the spring, laying about 100,000 eggs in a nesting season.

Smaller than peas, many just-laid horseshoe crab eggs (below) spill from their nests. Only eggs that remain buried in the sand develop. A horseshoe embryo (right) can be seen swimming in its bubble.

Soft and gooey when laid, the pearl-green eggs soon harden. They feel smooth if you roll them between your thumb and forefinger. One tiny egg could fit inside an O on this page. Sunshine and seawater keep the eggs warm and moist for 2 to 4 weeks in the sand.

For the first few days, horseshoe **embryos** grow unseen inside their green shells. But the eggs gradually swell until their outer shells burst. Each egg's inner covering is clear. Looking at an egg at this stage, you will see a tailless horseshoe embryo, turning, kicking, and swimming inside a crystal-clear bubble.

Although this year-old horseshoe crab is much smaller than the adult horseshoe it rests on, it looks like a miniature adult.

The growing embryo has a chitin shell, just like an adult, and chitin can't stretch as the embryo gets bigger. So the embryo must **molt,** or shed its chitin shell, four times inside the egg.

The clear eggshells soon split apart, and brand-new horseshoe crabs, called **larvae,** fill the nest. When the next high tide covers the beach, thousands of larvae wash into the bay.

The larvae swim upside down, paddling with their legs and book gills. But they don't swim far. After about a week, they settle to the bay bottom. Buried in soft, worm-rich mud, they can safely eat and eat—and grow.

After hatching, horseshoes molt five or six times in their first year. Year-old spike-tails are about as wide as half dollars and look like miniature adults. They still spend most of their time eating and growing in the mud.

The molted shell (on right) is smaller and lighter in color than the horseshoe crab's new shell (on left).

Before each molt, a soft, wrinkled shell forms inside the old one. Then the horseshoe burrows into the bottom muck for protection. The animal takes in water, swelling quickly, and the front edge of the cephalothorax splits. Soon a soft-shelled horseshoe crawls out of the old shell into the mud (true crabs back out of their shells when they molt).

The horseshoe then absorbs more water, expanding by about one-fourth.

Once the new shell hardens, it's safe for the animal to dig out of the mud.

Horseshoes molt several times a year during their first 3 years. The young animals crawl farther out to sea each year, spreading out from the beaches where they hatched. Horseshoes hatched in Delaware Bay can be found anywhere from New Jersey to Virginia, up to several miles offshore.

From age 3 on, horseshoes seem to molt only about once a year until they reach adulthood. It takes about 17 or 18 molts, or about 7 to 10 years, to become an adult ready to produce offspring. After this point, it's likely that neither males nor females ever molt again.

No one is sure exactly how long horseshoe crabs can live. Scientists, though, have found a clever way to estimate horseshoe life spans. A variety of small plants and animals—from sea lettuce and barnacles to tube worms and blue mussels—often attach themselves to a horseshoe's hard shell. One hitchhiker is the slipper snail, which may cling to an "undersea taxi" all its life. Researchers have found slipper snails up to 8 years old living on horseshoes. Thus, horseshoe crabs can live at least 8 years after their last molt—about 17 or 18 years total.

Slipper snails may spend their entire lives attached to a horseshoe crab.

Laughing gulls and shorebirds feast on horseshoe crab eggs.

A LINK IN A CHAIN

Every spring, hundreds of thousands of female horseshoes nest, each laying tens of thousands of eggs. Yet scientists estimate that fewer than 1 egg out of 130,000 survives to adulthood. What happens to all those eggs?

Fish dart under nesting females, snatching eggs as they drop into the water. Raccoons and foxes raid buried nests, and laughing gulls feed larvae to their chicks. Starlings, grackles, and gulls gobble the eggs littering the sand.

Over a million shorebirds descend on Delaware Bay each spring—tremendous flocks of red knots, ruddy turnstones, sanderlings, and several other species. The bay in springtime hosts the greatest population of migrating shorebirds in North America outside Alaska.

On Delaware Bay, though, many of the most colorful egg-eaters are travelers from afar. Red knots, ruddy turnstones, and other shorebirds are down to feather and bone when they arrive. These birds have burned up their body fat in spring migration, flying from their wintering grounds in Central and South America toward Arctic nesting grounds. To restore their fat reserves, they need to eat and eat.

What's the magnet that draws migrating flocks to Delaware Bay? Horseshoe crab eggs, of course! Bird food is scarce in spring along the Atlantic Coast. No other place on North America's East Coast offers such a rich and reliable food supply at the precise time the birds need it.

A migrating shorebird's marathon flight takes so much energy that the bird would die without such stopovers—safe places to rest with plenty of food. Each stopover is critical. It is a link in a chain of rest stops that keeps the birds alive.

With its short beak, a ruddy turnstone can reach only the top layer of eggs in a horseshoe crab's nest.

In truth, each tiny horseshoe egg has little food value. Worse, the hard-shelled eggs are tough to digest. So every shorebird must eat *lots*. A typical migrating shorebird devours about one egg every 5 seconds, 14 hours a day. Eating so heartily, it can double its weight in a 2-week bay visit.

The ruddy turnstone has such a great appetite for "horsefoot" eggs that it has earned the nickname "horsefoot plover." Using its special bill like a broom, a turnstone sweeps away the sand covering a horseshoe nest and begins its feast.

But its short beak can reach only the top eggs in each nest; then it moves on to open another hole. That gives longer-billed birds such as red knots and sanderlings their chance to dine.

At the peak of horseshoe nesting, birds along the Delaware Bay don't need to wait in line at egg holes. Horseshoe eggs are everywhere, carpeting the sand and sloshing in the waves. Eggs by the billion spill from nests because so many horseshoes lay eggs in the same narrow intertidal zone. Late-arriving horseshoes open old nests as they dig their own. The scattered eggs become a much-needed banquet for the birds.

By mid-June, though, Delaware Bay beaches are quieter and less colorful. Some horseshoes still lay eggs in the sand, but the great shorebird flocks have hurried north, their flight powered by energy from more than 300 tons of pearl-green horseshoe eggs.

Birds have no trouble finding horseshoe crab eggs at the height of nesting season on Delaware Bay.

GOOD-FOR-NOTHINGS?

Despite the many birds (and bird-watching tourists) that horseshoe crabs bring to the East Coast, not everyone thinks horseshoes are worth much. "Horsefeet!" sputter some fishers when horseshoes tangle their nets. "Good-for-nothing pests!" grumble many clammers, angry that horseshoes eat valuable shellfish.

These are not new complaints. In the early 1900s, clammers bashed horseshoe crabs with clam hoes or tossed them above the tideline to broil in the sun. Fishing towns offered rewards for dead horseshoes, so children on Cape Cod earned pocket money by collecting horseshoes for a few cents a tail. Beachcombers may still see spike-tailed shells littering the sand and wonder, "What good are they?"

The manner of their fishing.

Explorer John White made the first known sketch of a horseshoe crab in 1585, when he drew Algonquian people fishing near Roanoke Island.

Native Americans along the Atlantic Coast found many ways to use horseshoes. In the 1500s, Algonquian people on Roanoke Island (part of present-day North Carolina) tipped fishing spears with telsons of the animals they called *seékanauk*. Other native people used the shells as containers or as hand hoes for planting corn.

Native people may also have taught early settlers that adding chopped-up horseshoes to the soil helps crops grow. By the 1860s, a horseshoe crab fertilizer industry was booming. Horseshoes were handpicked off beaches, dried, and carted to factories for grinding. At the industry's peak in the late 1800s, over 4 million horseshoes were killed a year around Delaware Bay.

Captured horseshoe crabs (above) *are used as bait to catch eels* (right).

By the mid-1900s, though, the horseshoe fertilizer industry was shrinking. Neighbors of these factories wanted them shut down—they hated that smell! And farmers were turning to chemical fertilizers.

But fishers still caught some horseshoes to bait eel, whelk, and conch traps.

In about 1990, more and more people in Europe and Japan began eating conch and American eels, so more horseshoe crabs were picked off beaches and trawled from bay bottoms. Fishers who used to toss "pesky horseshoes" aside started catching and selling them for bait.

But some captured horseshoes end up in laboratories rather than in conch and eel traps. The hardy horseshoe is a nearly perfect laboratory animal—fascinating and easy to care for. Much has been learned about human biology and health by studying the horseshoe crab's eyes, nerves, and heart.

Researchers even study horseshoe crabs' chitin shells. Doctors in Japan have discovered that threads spun from chitin work better than silk for stitching wounds. A paste made from chitin is also being tested to fill cracks in broken bones. With so many uses for chitin, some people call it a "healing power from the sea."

Yet doctors value horseshoe crabs most of all for their blood. If you find a wounded horseshoe on the beach, you'll instantly spot its strange-looking blood. When the blood touches air, it turns blue!

The odd-colored blood has an amazing trait. It can detect bacteria (germs) and build a wall against them! Horseshoe blood has special blood cells that detect bacteria and **endotoxins,** the chemical poisons some bacteria make.

When these blood cells find bacteria or endotoxins, the blood immediately

Human blood looks red because it contains iron, and iron turns red, or "rusts," in the air. Horseshoes have copper in their blood that makes the blood turn royal blue in the air.

forms a **clot,** or thick plug, to stop the bacteria from invading. This simple protection system helps injured horseshoes stay healthy in seawater that's soupy with germs.

About 200,000 horseshoes are collected each year and shipped live to laboratories. A technician carefully inserts a needle into each animal and lets the blood drip into a bottle for a few minutes. Then the blue-blooded animals are returned alive to the water.

In the 1960s, scientists invented a test using horseshoe blood to detect endotoxins and bacteria in human medicines. Just a tiny amount of endotoxins in a person's bloodstream can cause dangerous fevers and even death. To test if a drug is clean of bacteria or endotoxins, the drug is mixed with an extract from horseshoe blood, called *Limulus* lysate. If a jellylike clot forms, the drug is not safe.

The *Limulus* lysate test is quick and can detect even the tiniest amount of endotoxins. It is used worldwide to check if medicines, blood donations, and medical supplies are clean and safe. Every year, the extraordinary blue bloods save thousands of human lives.

Scientists are counting fewer horseshoe crabs on some Atlantic Coast beaches.

LUCKY HORSESHOES?

Long before human beings even existed, horseshoe crabs thrived. After 360 million years on Earth, horseshoes may seem well armored against extinction. But there are signs of trouble.

On some beaches, fewer females are arriving each spring to lay eggs. What's happening to horseshoe crabs?

Some scientists blame the heavy use of horseshoes for eel and conch bait. Up and down the Atlantic Coast, hundreds of thousands of horseshoes are killed each year for bait. Scientists worry that horseshoe numbers will drop so low they could take decades to rise again.

Large rocks, placed along some beaches to protect buildings from waves, can cause horseshoes to get trapped and die.

Besides bait fishing, horseshoe crabs face another big threat: loss of nesting beaches. Along some beaches, thick walls have been built to protect buildings from waves. These walls shut out *Limuli* looking for places to nest. On beaches without walls, some communities toss rocks, broken cinder blocks, and bricks to slow sand loss. This junk doesn't stop horseshoes. But when they try to nest on the littered shores, they often get trapped and die.

Junk in the water causes problems as well. All along the Atlantic Coast, horseshoes live just offshore from cities as crowded and busy as New York. Sewage, factory waste, and rainwater carrying pollutants from parking lots, yards, and streets can kill clams and other animals that horseshoes depend on for food. Water pollution may also weaken or kill horseshoe eggs and larvae.

Fewer horseshoe crab eggs could mean that fewer shorebirds would reach their northern nesting grounds.

Will fewer horseshoe crabs and nests mean fewer migrating shorebirds?

Each spring, bird biologists make careful counts of Delaware Bay's feathered guests. Just as they have feared, flocks of several migrating species are shrinking.

Even more disturbing, scientists have evidence that the earth's climate is getting warmer. Many people believe the cause is too much carbon dioxide and other pollutants in the air. A warmer climate means warmer seawater, which could cause horseshoes to lay their eggs earlier in the spring. A change in the time of egg laying might break the link between nesting horseshoes and migrating shorebirds. Without plenty of eggs, the birds might not find enough other foods to make it to the Arctic to nest.

Worse still, warming temperatures might melt enough ice at the North and South Poles to raise the sea level. Many horseshoe nesting sites could vanish under the sea.

So what's being done to protect horseshoe crabs—and thus the birds? In 1991, Eastern Seaboard states started passing laws to limit the catch of horseshoes. In 1997, several states agreed to develop a coastwide plan to study and protect horseshoes. Yet many people feel additional efforts are needed.

Scientists contribute to horseshoe protection through research. Climate experts study how to slow down or stop global warming. Biologists attach numbered tags to horseshoes to track their undersea movements. Researchers also study hatching rates of horseshoes in polluted waters, and they replace sand on washed-out shores to learn if horseshoes will come back to nest.

Volunteers eagerly help with the research. Children and adults wade into the rising tide, clipboards in hand, marking down every male and female they see. Such nesting surveys help scientists learn how horseshoe numbers change from year to year.

Counting thousands of horseshoes is a big job. But when you watch hundreds of the helmet-shelled animals glistening in the moonlight or spy a flock of red knots overhead, all the work seems worthwhile.

Horseshoes may be common on some spring beaches, but they aren't the least bit "ordinary." Someday you may spot the ancient blue bloods nesting on a sandy shore. Stay a while, for you'll be witnessing the horseshoe crab continuing its extraordinary journey into the future.

GLOSSARY

abdomen: triangular-shaped midsection of a horseshoe crab

arthropods: animals with hard outer coverings, segmented bodies, and jointed legs but no backbones

book gills: breathing tissues of horseshoe crabs, where oxygen passes into blood through thin membranes that look like book pages

cephalothorax: the rounded front section of a horseshoe crab's body

chelicerae: first pair of pincers of a horseshoe crab or spider, used by horseshoes to grasp food

chitin: tough, horny material in the outer coverings of horseshoe crabs

claspers: special pincers shaped like boxing gloves on a male horseshoe crab's first pair of walking legs, used to grasp a female during mating

clot: a thick lump, formed when bacteria or endotoxins enter horseshoe crab blood

compound eyes: eyes made up of a number of separate light sensors

embryo: a young animal in the beginning stages of its development, before birth or hatching

endotoxins: poisons made by some kinds of bacteria which may cause illness if they enter an animal's blood

evolution: a slow process of change from an organism's original form to an organism's present form

extinct: having no members of a species left alive

gills: breathing organs of fish and many creatures that live underwater

intertidal zone: beach area between high and low tide waterlines

larvae: young of an organism that usually look very different from the adult form

molt: to shed outer covering, necessary for horseshoe crabs to grow

photoreceptors: light-sensitive cells that may occur alone or grouped together to form an eye

predators: animals that hunt and kill other animals for food

species: a kind of animal or plant

telson: the spikelike tail of a horseshoe crab

INDEX

ABOUT THE AUTHOR

Writer and naturalist **Julie Dunlap** turned her love for animals into a career. She earned a Ph.D. in Forestry and Environmental Studies at Yale University and wrote four biographies of scientists and environmentalists for children, including *Birds in the Bushes: A Story about Margaret Morse Nice,* also published by Carolrhoda Books. Horseshoe crabs captured her heart on a Delaware beach vacation with her husband and three children, Nathan, Hannah, and Sarah, who helped with the research for this book. The family lives in Columbia, Maryland.

Photos courtesy of: Tom Stack & Associates: © Joe McDonald, front cover, p. 24, © Brian Parker, back cover, © David M. Dennis, p. 8; © Photo Researchers: © Jeff L. Lepore, pp. 2, 28 (left), 31, 44–45, © Stephen J. Krasemann, pp. 4–5, © Vanessa Vick, pp. 7, 13, © Andrew J. Martinez, pp. 9 (left), 36, 38 (inset), 40, © James Hancock, p. 12 (top), © Virginia P. Weinland, p. 21 (inset), Francois Gohier, p. 26, © Kon Sasaki, p. 28 (right), © John Bova, p. 32, © Jim Zipp, pp. 33, 41, 43; Tony Stone Images: © Darrell Gulin, p. 6, © William L. Thomas, p. 9 (right), © Art Wolfe, p. 34; Bruce Coleman Inc.: © Ronald F. Thomas, p. 10 (left), © M. P. Kahl, p. 15 (top), © Joe McDonald, p. 15 (bottom), © David Overcash, p. 16, © Lynn M. Stone, p. 18, © Robert L. Dunne, p. 21 (top); © Norbert Wu, pp. 10 (right), 12 (bottom); Peter Arnold Inc.: © Fred Bavendam, p. 17, © Robert Villani, p. 35; © David W. Harp, pp. 19, 20, 27 (both), 29, 38 (top), 39, 42; © Dr. Robert Barlow, pp. 22 (both), 23; © Carl N. Shuster Jr., p. 30 (both); © The British Museum, p. 37; © Julie Dunlap, p. 48. Maps on pp. 11 and 25 by Lejla Fazlic Omerovic, copyright © 1999 Carolrhoda Books, Inc. Chart on p. 14 by University of Delaware Sea Grant Program.